SAMUEL BARBER

COMMEMORATIVE MARCH

Composed for Susie's (my sister's) wedding in my New York apartment —

for violin, violoncello, and piano
(score and parts)

Edited by David Flachs

On the cover:
A wedding photograph of Sarah Barber Beatty and Samuel Fulton Beatty
Pictured from left to right:
Samuel Barber, an unidentified woman, Sarah Barber Beatty, Samuel Fulton Beatty

ED 4463

First printing: November 2010

ISBN 978-1-6177-4263-7

G. SCHIRMER, Inc.
DISTRIBUTED BY
HAL•LEONARD®
CORPORATION
7777 W. BLUEMOUND RD. P.O. BOX 13819 MILWAUKEE, WI 53213

www.schirmer.com
www.halleonard.com

Samuel Barber composed "Commemorative March"
for the wedding of his sister Sarah ("Susie") to Samuel Fulton Beatty.
Sarah and Samuel were married on 4 May 1940
at the apartment of Samuel Barber and Gian Carlo Menotti,
166 East 96th Street, New York City.

duration ca. 2 minutes

The photograph of the wedding day for which this work was composed
was generously provided courtesy of Samuel Barber's niece and nephews,
the children of Sarah Barber Beatty and Samuel Fulton Beatty;
David Fulton Beatty
Christopher Fulton Beatty
Jeffrey Fulton Beatty
and
Judith Barber Beatty Taussig

Notes on the Edition

The manuscript facsimiles of the piano score and two string parts printed at the end of this edition are from the collection of the Library of Congress. The collection also includes an earlier sketch of this composition.

The only tempo indication which appears in all manuscripts printed in this edition is the "Poco Allegro" at measure 28. Barber provided no initial tempo for the work, therefore we have chosen a beginning tempo of ♪ = 84. All other tempo indications in the engraved edition are from the manuscript sources.

The piano score appears to have been copied quickly; it lacks the string parts in measure 30 and does not have a final barline. At measure 35 of the piano score, the notes for the strings are missing their stems, as are all notes in the last two measures. These notes are engraved as half notes as intended, not whole notes. For the most part, the dynamic indications were obtained from the manuscript of the violin part. The cello part is lacking dynamics for the last 10 measures of the work, therefore those found in the violin part have been duplicated for the cello. All dynamics for the piano are editorial estimations.

There is one pitch discrepancy in the existing sources of this work. In measure 5 of the manuscript piano score, the cello has the addition of a natural on the E, the 3rd note in the measure. This natural was obviously an added indication as a cautionary cancellation of the E sharp in the preceding measure. In the manuscript of the cello part, the copyist [Barber] wrote the note as E sharp however a natural was written over the sharp. We assume the cellist played this note as E natural and therefore it appears as E natural in the engraved score. Later, beginning in measure 19, the violin plays the same three measure phrase one octave higher. In measure 20, there is neither a sharp or natural in the violin line in the piano score and while the violin part itself has this note written as E sharp, there is no visible correction to indicate it was altered as was the cello part to make this E natural. We do not believe Barber intended the violin repetition of this phrase to be played differently by this one note. In the early sketch at the Library of Congress (which exists only in score form) this E in both passages contains neither a natural or sharp. Both passages have been engraved as E natural.

Commemorative March is catalogued as "H-98" in Barbara Heyman's *Samuel Barber: A Thematic Catalogue of the Complete Works.*

—David Flachs

COMMEMORATIVE MARCH

Composed for Susie's (my sister's) Wedding
in My New York Apartment

Samuel Barber

Largamente

Poco allegro

rit.

Composed for Susie's (my sister's)
wedding in my New York apartment

Commemorative March

Violin and
Violoncello

COMMEMORATIVE MARCH

*Composed for Susie's (my sister's) Wedding
in My New York Apartment*

Samuel Barber

Violin and
Violoncello

COMMEMORATIVE MARCH

Composed for Susie's (my sister's) Wedding
in My New York Apartment

Samuel Barber

Composed for Susie's (my sister's) wedding in my New York apartment —

piss

legatiss